GEORGE RHOADES

Along the
CHISHOLM
TRAIL
and Other Poems

outskirtspress

DENVER, COLORADO

Outskirts Press, Inc.
http://www.outskirtspress.com

ISBN: 978-1-4327-8499-7

Library of Congress Control Number: 2012905577

Outskirts Press and the "OP" logo are trademarks belonging to Outskirts Press, Inc.

PRINTED IN THE UNITED STATES OF AMERICA

Contents

PART ONE

Cowboys, Chisholm Trail

Along the Chisholm Trail

The cowboys who came up the trail,
Dusty, grimy, gritty, sweatin',
Drivin' the long, windin' herds,
Didn't know they were creatin'

A myth, a legend, shapin' a dream
For a nation and ridin' into history;
Epics, icons, symbols, heroic images
Emerged later to build the story.

They rounded up the wild longhorn,
Then pushed the beasts from down
Deep in the Texas brush country
North to the waiting Kansas cowtown.

The drama of those cattle drives,
Tales of horses and colorful men,
Reckless, free, brave, livin' outdoors —
Scenes never to be seen again.

No wonder the cowboys rode
Into the hearts and imagination
Of the world, and shaped forever
The endurin' character of this nation.

Spurs, chaps, ropes, saddles,
Six-shooters, wide hats, danger on the way,
On-the-move horses, big-horned cattle,
All ready-made for a show or stage play.

This energy and can-do attitude
Of the American cowboy on the trail
Sparked a massive outpourin'
From writers, poets, artists tellin' the tale.

Artists painted the dramatic images;
Russell, Remington and all the rest
Captured the color, the stunning splendor,
The mountains, valleys, plains of the West.

Wild west shows blossomed,
Dime novels were all the rage,
Early movie screens were full
Of cowboys of every age.

Fiction with sensational gunfights,
Desperadoes, cutthroats and outlaws,
Dashing heroic lawmen fighting
To bring order in a noble cause.

And the hard, grim reality
Of the cattle drive gave rise
To stories and pictures of sheer
Fantasy, invention and outright lies.

Billy the Kid, Kit Carson, Wild Bill,
Real characters of the frontier
Whose exploits were richly embellished,
As story and song began to appear

Of gaudy dress, fast draws, faster horses,
Yarns that boggled the mind,
From writers like Buntline and Grey
For the entertainment of all mankind.

Buffalo Bill's Wild West show
With cowboys, Indians, trick riders,
Ropers in sparklin' glitterin' garb
Thrilled audiences and filled coffers.

Shoutin', dashin', death-defyin'
Feats billed as life on the cattle drive,
Re-enacted amusements for throngs
Cheerin' as the West came alive.

Layer upon layer of romantic
Myth and legend shaped and coated
The cowboy story, which rodeo,
Movies, television all promoted.

Rodeo stars like Casey Tibbs,
Jim Shoulders and many more
Kept alive the wild and woolly days
With deeds that made the crowds roar.

Cowboys rode across the first
Movies that were ever made,
With Hoot Gibson, Tom Mix,
Who tackled bad guys unafraid.

William Hart, Gary Cooper, John Wayne,
Two-fisted, courageous and strong,
Roy and Gene, the singin' cowboys,
Galloped to stomp out any wrong.

The myth grew even stronger
Durin' the radio and television age,
Addin' to the expandin' grandeur
The cowboy era wrote on history's page

For the entertainment-seekin'
Masses who couldn't get enough
Of buckin' broncs, steer ropin',
And cowboys wild and tough.

The Golden Age of the Chisholm Trail
Lasted for only a short time,
But the impact on the nation
Rides on in story, picture and rhyme.

Billy the Kid

From Silver City to Lincoln County,
From the Rio Bonito to Mexico,
From the Sacramentos to the Hondo,
From Fort Sumner to Old Santa Fe,
The legacy and legend of Billy the Kid
Grew from desperate violent times,
Gave rise to myths, songs, rhymes
Embellishing the things that he did.

Billy's story gripped the nation
During an era of gunfighters in the West,
His deadly exploits topped all the rest,
And to this day a strong fascination
Still keeps his name and fame alive.
Although others killed more men
O'er longer outlaw careers back then,
The Kid's saga manages to thrive.

Was it because he died young
Or that he liked to laugh and dance
That made him a symbol of romance
When those violent tales are sung?
The real story is hard to find
About this slight, smiling youth;
Books, movies and lies hide the truth,
Which fabrication has intertwined.

They say he killed twenty-one,
But perhaps it was fewer than that;
He was in a "war," fierce combat,
Disputes settled with a blazing six-gun.
Billy was quick on the draw, no doubt,
Fast and accurate, showing little fear,
In those violent days of yesteryear,
Making his legend grow and stand out.

He tried to give up the outlaw trail,
But the governor refused to offer hope,
Left Billy to face the hangman's rope,
So he escaped from the Lincoln jail.
They had to kill him from ambush,
They couldn't do it face-to-face;
Being shot down in an isolated place,
Painted his fame with a broader brush.

So why did blue-eyed Billy become
The most famous gunfighter of all?
His name adorns street, dance hall,
Casino, museum and auditorium.
Perhaps it's really no deep mystery —
The Kid was an outlaw without peer
Facing down death with good cheer
To fulfill his gunsmoke destiny.

Cemetery

The little country cemetery clings to the hill,
Above the grassy slopes down below,
Silent, windswept, forlorn and weathered,
Through rain, sun, sleet and snow.

Keeping watch where the cattle herds once
Trailed up from Texas long, long ago;
Old tombstones leaning, barely staying upright,
Crowded by weeds, visited by coyote and crow.

In a lonely neglected corner
Stands a worn and crumbling stone,
The name obscure and unreadable,
And his story largely unknown.

In that remote piece of ground,
Forgotten are the lives of those at rest,
But at least one buried there took part
In a legendary epic of the West.

The pony engraved beside his name
Surely must've been his pride and joy,
And he's remembered with these words:
"A Chisholm Trail Cowboy."

Chisholm Trail Annie

The CA herd had crossed the Red,
And was bedded down for the night
Near the plateau called Lookout Point;
Nightriders circled, keepin' 'em quiet.

Dark clouds crawled from the south,
Rumblin' thunder, flashes of lightnin',
Longhorns were alert, nervous — tension
Built like a spring slowly tightenin'.

A brilliant dazzlin' bolt of fire
Struck in the middle of the restless herd,
And three thousand head swiftly leaped
To their feet in one motion undeterred.

Rain came sweepin' down as the storm
Exploded with howlin' fierce fury;
The great mass of animals at once
Ran like a wild angry rollin' sea.

Cowboys in the saddle ridin' hard
Amid the lightnin', thunder, rain
Tryin' to turn the steers in the lead
In a mad race o'er the rugged plain.

Gopher holes, gullies and ravines
Threatened the shoutin' cowboys,
Ridin' at a dead run in the dark,
Surrounded by horns, storm, noise.

"Trust your horse," old cowboys said,
But skill and bravery were put to the test
As the herd thundered into the inky black,
Lightnin' flashes showin' glimpses at best.

Shorty and Billy Joe ridin' hell for leather
Outside the stampedin' column of cattle
Tryin' to turn the leaders into a circle
To end the runnin' dangerous battle.

Herds can run for miles and scatter,
Hundreds can die fallin' o'er a bank,
Or into a draw or creek in their rush,
If riders don't get around their flank.

Gettin' 'em in a mill was the only way
To bring the avalanche under control;
The cowboys knew their horses' next jump
Could bring their final earthly toll.

Shorty and Billy Joe swore they saw
In the flashes on the ridge ahead,
A slender girl rider turnin' the leaders
From runnin' into a tight circle instead.

The millin' herd slowly settled down,
And the two cowpokes rode up to the girl;
They said she had dark flowin' hair
And her pony was pale as a pearl.

She said her name was Annie,
And she was glad to help them out;
When they turned back she was gone,
But they swore she was there no doubt.

None of the other drovers saw her,
And shook their heads at the story
Told by the two riders about the girl;
They dismissed it as exaggerated oratory.

Shorty and Billy Joe wondered to themselves:
Was it all just invention and fantasy
What they had seen on the ridge that night?
Was she real — this Chisholm Trail Annie?

Later ridin' back down to South Texas,
The boys stopped at Fleetwood, where
They asked if anybody knew about
A girl named Annie with dark flowin' hair.

The tale they were told was startlin':
That a girl named Annie died years ago
Out on the prairie near Lookout Point
When cattle stampeded off the plateau.

Shorty and Billy Joe kept quiet
And didn't talk much at all eventually,
When they were asked about the stampede,
And the mysterious Chisholm Trail Annie.

Crossin' the Red

We pushed 'em to the Red,
And the trail boss said,
"We're gonna cross the river here;
Crowd 'em in, have no fear."

Reluctant cowhands told the boss,
"It seems a bad place to cross;
Shouldn't we scout down the line,
Look for a better trail and crossin' sign?"

"This is the best place to go,
In my heart of hearts, I know;
You gotta have more faith and grit,
So, boys, gird it up and get with it."

"But, boss, maybe there's quicksand,
Undertow, drop-offs, whirlpools and
Steep, muddy banks on the other side,
Plus right here seems to be too wide."

"Have faith and grit, and run 'em in,
Boys, run 'em in, and let's begin
To get this herd into the water.
We need to swim 'em faster and faster."

Half the herd was lost in the river.
Three cowboys and the trail boss never
Came out on the other side alive
To finish the ill-fated cattle drive.

Faith and grit are great to have,
But when temptin' fate and the grave,
'Tis wise to check and check again
Before blindly runnin' 'em in.

Drover's Moon

The cowboy said,
"I'll see you soon,
When I come back
'Neath the drover's moon."

She pleaded and cried,
"Please don't go
On another trail drive,
I miss you so.

"I'm so afraid
You'll not return
From another drive's
My main concern."

He left her there
Near the Brazos green
And trailed the herd
On to Abilene.

She waited for him.
The months went by
From Spring to Fall
Soft as a sigh.

The big bright moon
Rode through the sky
When nights were clear
And weather dry.

Some herders didn't
Come back again,
After the journey
To the railroad pen.

Stampede and flood,
And snakebite, too,
Took their toll
On quite a few.

Some cowpunchers
Met their fate
In the wild towns
In Kansas state.

Comanche raiders
And other peril
Left grave markers
Beside the trail.

She waited and waited.
Her heart was breakin',
Workin' on the farm,
Feelin' forsaken.

The drover's moon
Floated on high
When he came ridin'
Back by and by.

"I've had enough,"
The cowboy said,
"All I want's
My home and bed.

"No more long drives,
Never'd be too soon,"
He swore to her
'Neath the drover's moon.

Farm for Sale

The old handbill tattered and faded;
Memories across my mind paraded,
Recalled a time and told the tale,
Proclaimed for all "Farm for Sale."

Back when my mom and dad
Sold almost everything they had,
Moved us into a little town,
Givin' up, gettin' out, worn down.

F-30 Farmall tractor and hay baler,
Coal oil heater, two-row cultivator,
Sows and pigs and horses, too,
A way of life finally through.

Jersey cows, bull and steers,
Stuff gathered o'er the years
Strugglin' tryin' to make a livin',
Crop failures, poverty unforgivin'.

Gasoline barrels, cream separator,
Two-bottom plow and Case thresher,
Harness, bridles and saddle,
Ropes and headgate for cattle.

Spring tooth harrow, cotton planter,
Seven-foot mower and ten-foot binder,
Six-foot combine, 300 hay bales,
Tools and wires and set of scales.

I remember it all back then,
We made the move when I was ten;
Leavin' behind the old home place
For a different tread, a different pace.

Noisy neighbors right next door,
Rural solitude lost forevermore;
Indoor plumbing and electric lights,
No more dark and silent nights.

My dad took a job, earned a wage,
Said it felt like livin' in a cage;
We often talked about long-gone days,
Never really lost our country ways.

Mom was tearful but resigned
To leavin' the country life behind;
"It'll be better," is what she said.
"We've got to move on and look ahead."

A 16-hole McCormick drill,
One Sears-Roebuck hammer mill;
No more walkin' two miles to school,
No more perched on a milkin' stool.

No more chicks and gatherin' eggs,
No more garden or sloppin' pigs;
Little crowded house, pinched city lot,
Somehow a smaller, shrunken spot.

No more pastures of our own,
No more timber, hill and rocky stone,
No more huntin' our own land;
We ask permission now, hat in hand.

Two-row go-devil, six-foot one-way,
White-face calves and hatchin' tray,
The old handbill, crumblin' and brown;
We sold out and moved to town.

Chicken coops and butane brooder,
Fruit jars and cannin' cooker,
Hammers, hoes, saws and rakes,
Building blocks, posts and stakes.

All those things and many more
Auctioned off by the score,
Bought and gone before sundown,
When we sold the farm, moved to town.

Guns

Tex was an avid gun collector,
Various pistols and rifles galore,
Colts, Smith and Wessons, Remingtons,
Plus a special group of rare handguns
He cleaned and polished every day
Much to his wife's dismay.

"You love your guns more'n me,"
She complained and whined bitterly.
Tex denied that was true, but resolved
One thing about guns he really loved.
Tex with a smirk said to her,
"On a gun you can put a silencer."

Horseback Ridin'

Horseback ridin', studies show,
Is really great, don't you know,
Builds muscles and clears the mind,
Toughens your endurance and behind,
Burns calories along the way,
Great activity to start the day.
The studies are right, all in all,
Except for muckin' out the stall.

How Hot and Dry Was It?

We was settin' around the campfire,
The herd all quiet and bedded down,
Shootin' the breeze like cowboys do,
Listenin' for nightriders to circle round.

The boys started tellin' tales about
How hot and dry it had been.
I jotted down some of the things
They recalled from way back when.

I'd heard some of the sayin's before,
And they've been repeated quite a bit,
But here's some of what they said,
A sampler of Texas fabrication and wit:

It was hotter'n a stolen tamale,
Lizards walked on stilts for legs,
It was drier'n the inside of a haystack,
And the chickens laid hard-boiled eggs.

Frogs jumped in the fryin' pan to cool off,
Dogs were chased by the mesquite trees,
Birds used potholders to pull up worms,
And it was so dry, catfish had fleas.

When it rained 40 days and 40 nights,
West Texas got a quarter of an inch,
And cows were givin' powdered milk,
Which worked just dandy in a pinch.

So dry, the Baptists started sprinklin',
Catholics were tryin' to turn the wine
Back into water, and the Methodists
Swore cactus juice worked just fine.

One year, an old cowpoke recalled,
It kept on gettin' drier and drier
Until out west beyond the Pecos,
Birds built nests usin' barb wire.

Rabbits were carryin' water bags,
And when they finally had a Norther,
Sandstorms were called Panhandle Showers,
And dust devils danced with each other.

Buzzards were flyin' backwards to keep
Sand outta their eyes and beat the heat;
It got so hot Texans pulled up taters
Fully baked, ready to butter and eat.

The Devil came out for a tour,
But didn't stay too long, legends tell,
He scurried right back to Hades
'Cause West Texas was hotter'n Hell.

In the Nursing Home

Poppa, you'll like it here
Inside the nursing home
Now that Momma's gone
And you're livin' all alone.

We've sold your tractor,
Leased out all the land,
Cleared the house and barn;
We hope you'll understand.

You won't have to walk
Past the cedars to the spring,
Or work in the garden
When birds are on the wing.

You've got your own room,
TV, games and dining hall,
Lots of people all around
To answer when you call.

No more livin' way out there
With the wind blowin' free
Across the flowers in the field
Where you watched the honeybee.

You won't have to be alone
While the fiery evenin' sun
Fades away below the hills
Where the ponies used to run.

And you won't have to spend
Your days down at the creek
Worryin' about bait and hook
When the skies are cold and bleak.

So, Poppa, you'll like it here
Inside the nursing home
Now that Momma's gone
And you're livin' all alone.

In Troubled Times

In troubled times
Like these today,
We need to remember
The Cowboy Way.

Standin' firm,
Not backin' down;
Doin' what's right
With nary a frown.

Givin' your word
And meanin' it, too,
When shufflin' off
Is easier to do.

Tryin' your best
To get 'er done,
No matter how tough
Or long the run.

Make things better;
Do what you can
To improve the lives
Of your fellow man.

We've been down
Rough roads before
And come through
Hard times and war.

We have a guide
To show us how
To get past troubles
Like we have now.

So we should remember
Every single day
To keep followin'
The Cowboy Way.

Isabella

Isabella cried and cried
The day he rode away
To join the cattle drive
Headed north that very day.

"I'll wait for you," she said,
"Right here forever and ever
Along the flowery banks
Of the Guadalupe River."

The cowboy helped take
The herd through ragin' storm,
Flood, stampede and danger
To the Kansas train platform.

The long days were hot and dusty,
The nights seemed without end,
Pushin' the longhorn herd
O'er prairie land and river bend.

The cowboy kept rememberin'
What his Isabella had said
The day he left her there
Her words soundin' in his head.

"I'll wait for you," she said,
"Right here forever and ever
Along the flowery banks
Of the Guadalupe River."

Bluebonnets were all abloom
When he joined the trail crew,
And when he rode home again
Summer was nearly through.

Cholera had swept the land
While he had been gone
Takin' Isabella and many others,
Leavin' the cowboy all alone.

A tiny cross marked the spot
In the shade 'neath the trees
Where her grave had been placed
To catch the evenin' breeze.

"I'll wait for you," she said,
"Right here forever and ever
Along the flowery banks
Of the Guadalupe River."

Jesse

I think that it's kinda funny,
Or with at least a bit of irony,
That Jesse Chisholm never knew
His name would be forever linked to
The greatest cattle trail of them all,
Creating legend and song to enthrall
The nation and the world, too,
With tales of cowboy derring-do.
There's one thing, it seems to me,
To learn from the story of Jesse:
I guess you never know what kind
Of legacy you might leave behind,
Or what sort of lasting fame
Might become attached to your name.

Maggie Belle
and
The Yeller Moon Saloon

Maggie Belle was a buxom gal,
Flame-haired and eyes of green;
She ran the Yeller Moon Saloon
On a dusty street in Abilene.

'Twas a favorite waterin' place
For thirsty Texas cowhands
Who brought half-wild longhorns
Up from southern grasslands.

The Yeller Moon had dancin' girls,
Hard liquor and gamblin' tables, too,
A piano player and a fiddler,
And a "lady of the evenin'" or two.

Maggie Belle and her bouncers
Kept strict order night and day,
And she was adept and skillful
At holdin' the cowboys at bay.

She carried a long hatpin,
Plus a two-shot silvery derringer
Tucked inside her ample bosom,
A mighty handy discourager.

That's why it was a surprise
When she fell for Kerrville Slim,
Lanky, awkward and kinda shy,
Couldn't keep her eyes offa him.

Arizona Bill was big and mean.
He carried six-shooters and a knife,
And he bragged to one and all
That Maggie Belle'd be his wife.

He had notches on his gun,
And most learned to step aside,
'Cause Arizona Bill when riled
Was rough and tough as rawhide.

But Maggie Belle told him quick
She didn't want him at all,
That her and Kerrville Slim
Might tie the knot in the fall.

One dark night at the Yeller Moon
Bill warned Slim to stay away
From Maggie Belle or it'd be
His final final judgment day.

Bill, totin' ivory-handled guns,
Told Slim he'd meet him at noon
For a man-to-man showdown
In front of the Yeller Moon Saloon.

Friends told Slim he'd better
Git on back down to Kerrville,
Stay on the ranch he owned there,
And forget all about Maggie Belle.

But Slim swore he wouldn't run,
And said he was gonna meet
Arizona Bill and his deadly guns
For a shoot-out in the Abilene street.

Of course, Bill didn't show up
'Cause they found him shot dead
Back of the Yeller Moon Saloon,
Two bullet holes in his head.

The sheriff said it was strange,
And a case that truly mystifies
How somebody got close enough
To shoot Bill between the eyes.

Slim and Maggie Belle, they say,
Tied the knot real soon,
Moved down to the Texas ranch,
Leavin' behind the Yeller Moon Saloon.

Mesquite

All o'er the Southwest
You'll find tough things
With horns and thorns
And claws and fangs.

There's diamondback rattlers,
Stingin' scorpions that bite,
Prickly pear and javelinas,
Tarantulas crawlin' at night.

The sun's hot as fire,
Rain scarce and sparse,
The terrain inhospitable,
Livin' conditions harsh.

Early cowboys all said
The wild rangy and mean
Longhorn was the toughest
Thing they'd ever seen.

Some say the horns,
Wider'n an open gate,
Are the perfect symbol
For the Lone Star State.

But the toughest of all
Has really got to be
The "Texas Iron-Wood,"
The dense mesquite tree.

Thrivin' and growin'
Where nothin' else will,
Often only a bush
Almost impossible to kill.

Tenacious and persistent,
Called the rancher's curse,
For ruinin' grasslands
Nothin' could be worse.

Millions of acres
From Texas to Arizona
Coverin' prairie and mesa
On out to California.

From a shrub to a tree
Up to 60 feet tall,
The mighty mesquite,
Sturdy as a stone wall,

Puts down roots
Almost 200 feet deep
To find cool moisture
'Neath the dry desert heat.

Indians used the beans
For a food supply;
Its charcoal adds taste,
No cook can deny.

Furniture is made
From its hard wood,
And the first pioneers
Used whate'er they could.

Gnarly and crooked,
The durable branches
Provided posts for fences,
Houses for ranches.

Mesquites surely define
Rugged individuality,
Toughness and stubbornness,
As well as adaptability

Of the people who settled
The area where it grows
From the Southern Plains
To the arid plateaus.

The most perfect icon
That can't be beat
To mark the Southwest
Has to be the mesquite.

Monument Hill

Monument Hill,
Old memories still
Linger there
Fillin' the air.
Maybe 'tis true
That places do
Absorb sensations,
Capture vibrations
From things
And happenings
Of long ago;
And we know
In some strange way
Events that replay
In our senses
That reason dismisses.

The marker stands
Where trail hands
Bedded down at night
'Neath the moonlight,
Pushin' the big herds
Ever northwards.
You can almost feel,
Seems somehow real,
The reflections
And recollections
Along the plateau
And down below,
Left behind
All intertwined
In memory
And history.

My Daddy Is A Cowboy

She was just barely three,
Holding to her mother's hand,
Blue eyes lookin' up at me
At the museum's front door stand.

"My daddy is a cowboy;
Are you a cowboy, too?"
Her tiny voice full of joy
Fresh as the mornin' dew.

"I sure would like to be,"
Was all that I could say;
Her laughter a happy melody
As she hurried on her way.

She knew that it was good
To be a "cowboy" somehow —
I wondered how she understood
Those distant days even now,

Back when they crossed the Red
Pushin' hard, pointin' 'em North,
A herd of two thousand head
Movin' on, past old Fort Worth,

Through rain, wind and hail,
And worse all along the way,
Drivin' up the Chisholm Trail
Near where we stand today.

Museum, statue and monument
Mark those days of long ago,
But the real lastin' testament
That doesn't always show

Was captured in the glee,
And the little girl's happy joy
As she laughed up at me,
"My daddy is a cowboy."

Not His
First Rodeo

The cowboys were leanin'
On the rodeo arena gates
When up drove this old truck
With New Jersey plates.

The truck was old and rusty,
Smokin' and motor knockin',
Tires bald and threadbare,
Frame swayin' and rockin'.

It rolled to a noisy stop,
Brakes squawkin' and squealin',
And out stepped a cowpoke
Whose attire seemed revealin'.

Dusty crumpled old hat,
Boots scuffed and worn out,
Ragged tattered denim shirt,
Torn jeans left no doubt,

'Twas a seasoned wrangler,
Or it really appeared so,
'Cause the words he said were:
"This ain't my first rodeo."

He said he'd paid his fee,
Speakin' with a funny accent,
And he was in the bull ridin',
Which was his favorite event.

The boys called him Jersey,
Said they'd like to know
More about him, and he said,
"This ain't my first rodeo."

Jersey didn't tell 'em much,
Hinted that he used to ride
For a big ranchin' spread
Out along the Great Divide.

So the boys were watchin'
Jersey to see how it went
When he took part
In the bull ridin' event.

Buckin' broncs, ropin' horses,
Bulldoggin', barrel races,
Cowboys and cowgirls
Goin' through their paces.

Jersey's turn finally came.
He was ridin' ole Hacksaw,
A ton of twistin' dynamite,
One of the worst of the draw.

The cowboys offered Jersey
Friendly advice on how to ride,
But he shook his head,
Calmly took it all in stride.

With his braided bullrope
Firmly wrapped in place,
In his scruffy leather chaps
And a scowl on his face,

Jersey eased onto Hacksaw,
Pulled his hat down low,
Wrapped his hand real tight,
As if he'd made the short go.

Jersey had told the boys
Just a short time ago,
Said it clear once more,
"This ain't my first rodeo."

Jersey raised his free hand,
Nodded to open the chute,
And Hacksaw exploded out,
A buckin', spinnin' brute.

Hacksaw's head was down,
Hind legs kickin' high,
The crowd was on its feet,
Cheers reachin' for the sky.

With the bull's first jump,
Jersey's hat went one way,
And he went sailin' t'other,
The worst ride of the day.

He hit the arena floor,
Skidded through the dust,
The clowns to the rescue,
Crowd moaned in disgust.

They loaded Jersey in the van,
Got him to the medics,
Who said he'd be okay,
Despite some nasty licks.

As they were pickin' Jersey up,
Thinkin' it was touch and go,
They heard him softly mutter,
"This *was* my first rodeo."

Old Men
At the Coffee Shop

Pickups out front in a row,
Like horses tied to the rail,
At the little country diner
Slightly off the beaten trail.

Truck beds are all cluttered
With shovels, posts and wires,
Stretchers, diggers, old gas cans,
Blocks of salt, worn-out tires.

Old men gathered early
At a table way in the back,
"Swappin' lies are you?"
Draws a quick comeback.

Someone younger passing says,
"Solved all the problems yet?"
And several gravelly voices
Call a stern reply, "You bet!"

This early morning ritual
Old men drinkin' coffee,
Tellin' tales 'bout the weather,
The way things used to be.

'Bout things they've done,
And things they haven't done,
Things they have lost
And races they have won.

Worn and wrinkled gimme caps,
Cowboy hats, calloused hands,
Workin' always close to home,
Or followin' oil to far-off lands.

Ups and downs, births and deaths,
Triumphs and tragedies endurin',
Stories told and oft repeated,
'Bout growin' up and maturin'.

Choices made and forced to make,
Regrets, remorse and laughter, too,
Along the trails they have ridden
As journey's end comes in view.

Old Sam and Penny

The old cowboy, Sam was his name,
Used to ride his paint horse, Penny,
Around the community farm to farm
Visitin', talkin', friendly as can be.

Sam had a stroke when he was seventy,
And couldn't drive his old Model T,
But he could saddle and ride the mare,
Though he couldn't do it easily.

Penny would stand while he saddled up,
And she always came when he called her;
He'd had her from a colt years ago,
Never had to use a rope, whip or spur.

Sam's story like that of many others,
Not exceptional or uncommon or unusual,
Workin' hard, helpin' settle the land,
Takin' part in events mundane and historical.

When the cattle drives faded away,
Sam ran the Cherokee Strip in '93.
He staked out a farm, but didn't stay
Long enough to get a deed clear and free.

By 1901 in the Oklahoma land lottery,
He had a farm, plus a wife and family,
Settled down to plow the ground,
Raisin' kids, crops, cows persistently.

The kids grew up and moved away,
His wife died and left him all alone;
He stayed on the farm doin' his best
Livin' in the old house, strugglin' on.

For years, Penny was his companion
Standin' untied waitin' patiently
As he rode to the country store
Or to visit old pals frequently.

Sam's health finally went downhill,
And he would rest in his bedroom,
Starin' out the window at Penny
Grazin' where the wildflowers bloom.

The old cowboy was nearin' 90
The day he passed away in bed.
Friends, relatives gathered at the farm
Found Penny lyin' in the meadow dead.

Ole Red
And
The Lawman

She was wild-eyed and mean,
And we called her Ole Red —
Rangy, rawboned and lean,
Wicked horns on her head.

Every rancher has one or
more —
Cows that run and shy away,
Handlin' them's a nasty chore
When it comes to loadin' day.

She'd spook the other cattle,
And drivin' 'em to the pen
Would turn into a major battle
Before we got 'em shut in.

Tossin' her head, bawlin' loud,
Hookin' and pushin' all the
others;
That's when Herbie vowed
To sell, if he had his druthers.

Neighbors came from all
around
With horses in the mix
To get Ole Red run to ground
Using all their cowboy tricks.

We finally got her in the chute
With curses, punches, cattle
prod,
Lariat, lash, whip and boot;
Herbie shut the gate with a
nod.

Ole Red put up quite a show
Bangin' the sides of Herbie's
truck,
Almost like a one-cow rodeo,
But now if we had any luck,

We'd get her safely to the sale
Scheduled that very
afternoon,
Then let her kick and flail,
For us it wouldn't be too soon.

On the highway we heard a
sound
And we stopped, got out to
find
Ole Red was tryin' to get
around
Sideboards that had her
confined.

Ole Red was hangin' near half
out.
We pushed and shoved her
back in,
And to see what we were about
A patrolman stopped, flashed
a grin.

This trooper, sharp as he
could look
In hat, jacket, and shirt all
pressed,
Walked up with his ticket
book
Ready to write what we
guessed

Would be a warning designed
to keep
The roads and highways all
secure
From raggedy, dirty, smelly,
cheap
Cowpokes half covered in
manure.

And since we're speakin' of
manure
That's when Ole Red let fly
With fecal matter most
impure.
Splotches hit the uniform and
tie —

He brushed at them with his
hand,
And departing said, "Have a
nice day."
As if he'd simply planned
To chat and then be on his
way.

Ole Red brought a dandy
price,
And despite all the
consternation,
Let's just say it was suffice —
She did prevent some traffic
irritation.

Restin' Place

I came up from South Texas
Where the bluebonnets grow,
Followin' the longhorns north
Swayin' in the saddle to and fro.

Through brush hills and rollin' plains,
Crossin' tricklin' streams and river flood,
Dusty, weary, bone-tired at end of day,
Swirlin' dirt and sweat and quicksand mud.

I rode 'round the herd at night
When the stars shone like dots of fire,
And the moon floated on velvet black,
Wind soft, whisperin' a nightly choir.

I listened to the meadowlarks
And watched the hawks on the wing,
Breathed the sage-perfumed air
Ridin' through the flowerin' spring.

I watched the sunrise at morn,
And the dyin' rays at fiery sunset,
Crowded 'round the chuck wagon
For the beans and beef banquet.

But I won't see my home again,
My momma or the girl I left behind;
At eighteen I joined the cattle drive
To see what adventure I could find.

On the banks of the wild Cimarron,
I found my final restin' place,
'Neath a wooden cross and rough stone,
Wrapped in the prairie's cold embrace.

Scatter My Ashes

Scatter my ashes along the trail,
Let the prairie winds blow free,
Let the rain and sun, snow and hail
Come down over me.

That's where I want to be,
Where the great cattle drives
Passed into history,
And only memory survives.

I want to mingle with the dust
Under the wide and starry sky,
Remember me if you must—
A cowhand from days gone by.

Don't sing a sad song
When I cross the Great Divide,
I'll be ridin' where I belong,
Where cowboy spirits abide.

Sounds
Of the Trail

Sometimes late at night
When the wind blows just right
Across the ridge through the trees
Sounds come driftin' with the breeze;
Sounds of the trail fill the darkness
Floatin' around in the quietness,
Sounds left from long, long ago
When cattle herds were on the go
Movin' north to the Kansas rail,
Movin' on up the Chisholm Trail.

Saddles creakin' and cattle bawlin',
Shufflin', restless, with coyotes howlin',
Old cowhands singin' soft lullabies
'Neath the shinin' moon and starry skies,
Maybe "Old Paint" or "The Zebra Dun"
To settle 'em down after the sun
Slides below the hills to the west,
Low voices keepin' longhorns at rest,
Nightbirds addin' their clear call,
Calm, serene, soothin' to all.

"Red River Valley" or "Cowboy's Lament,"
Cowboys addin' verses as they went
Round and round the bedded-down herd
Soft and gentle as a callin' bird.
Listen real close and you'll hear
Those sounds comin' from yesteryear,
Driftin' down o'er the vast prairie,
Recallin' the past in dreamy reverie.

Thank God
For the Grass

Plains, bluestem, short and tall,
Alfalfa, bermuda and
Johnson, too,
Grasses of all kinds and
shapes
More than enough for a
harvest crew.

Newly cut giant round bales
Scattered, waiting, I like to see
Before they're moved off
somewhere
Seem somehow comfortin' to
me.

Much better'n little square
ones
We used to load and "buck"
by hand,
Tote and stack inside the barn
When summer roasted the
land.

Fat plump bales are like a sign
That means another harvest's
done,
The grass supply now
protected
When wintertime starts its run.

The poverty line might be
nearby,
But the bales seem to make
the plea
That the grasses growin' far
and wide
Point the way to prosperity.

Ranchin's real foundation
key,
The stuff that makes it come
to pass,
Is blessed in the old
benediction:
"Thank God for the grass."

The Cowboy Way

We've all heard about The Cowboy Way:
Stand yer ground, don't give in,
Do the best with what you've got,
Tall in the saddle, loyal to a friend.

Hard roads, hard knocks, hard goin',
The cowboy cinches up, gets on with it,
Stands by his word, means what he says,
Faces down adversity with courage and grit.

But it's also helpin' the needy,
Givin' a hand to those downtrodden,
The unfortunate, the poor and homeless,
The heavy-laden and the forgotten.

It's more'n just bein' strong
And tough and rugged day after day,
Compassion's also what it means
To say, "Cowboy Up—The Cowboy Way."

The Devil
And the Fast Gun

Albert Fink was a cattle rustler,
A petty thief and a cheap con man,
And sometimes a crooked gambler
Way down along the Rio Grande.

But he wanted to be known
All around as the fastest gun,
Whose presence in the town
Would strike fear in everyone.

Albert knew all the names
Of the gunfighters of the day,
From Billy the Kid to Jesse James,
And others too numerous to say.

He'd practice with his forty-four
In a hideout where he'd go,
Slappin' leather o'er and o'er,
But he knew he was still too slow.

One day out lookin' for some steers
To drive from the herd and steal,
Albert had to overcome his fears
Chasin' cattle into Satan's Heel.

Satan's Heel was a rugged outcroppin'
Far out on the brush-covered range,
Where cowpokes didn't care for stoppin'
'Cause of stories scary and strange.

Old Satan hisself had been said
To appear out there once in a while,
Horns and tail and eyes bloodred,
Hissin' and swearin' oaths most vile.

Sure enough from behind a rock,
The Devil popped up, tossed a rope,
Caught Albert in a brimstone lock
Drug him kickin' down a cactus slope.

"I'll make you the fastest gun ever,"
Satan said when he saw who he had,
"And you'll be remembered forever
As the very baddest of the bad.

"But your soul's gonna be mine,"
The Devil told Albert with a grin;
Albert agreed that was just fine,
If he'd be the fastest there's ever been.

Albert strode to the Mesquite Saloon
Wearin' his Colt low on his hip
The very next day just at noon,
Bellyin' up to the bar for a nip.

"I'm the fastest gun of all,"
Albert sneered at the dusty cowboys,
Who wondered at his foolish gall
'Cause at the bar was Ben Lajoys.

Ben Lajoys had a mighty fast draw,
A man with 20 notches on his gun,
The best the folks here ever saw
At puttin' wannabes on the run.

Albert and Ben met in the street
And went for their guns at once —
Albert went down to dyin' defeat,
Victim of fast-gun incompetence.

Next Albert was appearin' afore
A dancin' and prancin' old Nick,
Waitin' to open Hell's fiery door,
And laughin' hisself almost sick.

"You tricked me," Albert cried,
"I wasn't the fastest gun, for sure."
"That's right," Satan cruelly replied,
"I wanted you quick and secure.

"So now I've got your soul,
But I was gonna get it anyway.
You'll have to pay a heavy toll
For the evil you did durin' your day.

"You knew I was the Devil
When you made that pact with me;
There's no way I was on the level,
And I lie most frequently."

The James Boys' Buried Treasure

Rumors and legends abound
About treasure hidden away
In the granite-clad Wichitas,
Still unfound to this day.

The James boys, it is said,
Buried loot in Cut Throat Gap,
And in other remote places
Marked on a cowhide map.

Frank and Jesse ran rampant
Throughout the hills and plains
Of Missouri and other states
Robbing coaches, banks and trains.

Years after Jesse died,
Frank moved to Fletcher town,
Spent several years prowlin'
The mountains up and down.

Frank wore out six horses
Durin' that time, so they say,
Ridin' and diggin' all around,
Not findin' much to tote away.

One tale tells about the time
The James gang robbed a Kansas bank,
Fled south into the Wichitas,
Hidin' in a cave cold and dank.

Desperate law officers hired
The Pinkerton Detective Agency
In an effort to put an end
To the outlaw gang's depravity.

Three-Finger Dan was an agent
Who tried to track them down.
Dan was known far and wide,
Persistent as an old bloodhound.

Now Dan and his deputies
Were in hot pursuit on their trail
After banks were robbed in Iowa,
Plus trains haulin' the U.S. mail.

Stagecoaches held up in Texas,
Then the bank in Dodge City,
The Pinkertons chased the gang
To the best of their ability.

But the James boys got away
In the Wichitas' rugged fastness,
And the stories say the loot
Was buried in the rocky vastness.

Tryin' to find the buried treasure,
Dan searched on all alone.
Frank came back years later,
But apparently the money was gone.

Maybe it was just a tall tale,
But it remains a mystery.
Treasure hunters still show up
Ready to dig, eager as can be.

They say Dan quit the Pinkertons,
Moved down south to relocate
On a sprawlin' ranch he bought
Deep in the heart of the Lone Star state.

The Newspaper

The old newspaper has shut its doors,
Closed, out of business, rest in peace;
Silent after all these years,
Empty building marked, "For Lease."

It began in those long-gone days
In back of a store, beside a jail
Where the half-wild longhorns
Were driven up the Chisholm Trail.

The founding editor had come West
With type, ink, paper and press
Loaded onto a covered wagon,
Stopped where his best guess

A community would take root.
Churches, shops, schools for a town
That looked like it could become
A place for folks to settle down.

Type set by hand filled the weekly;
News of fires, politics, shootin's,
Clubs, gossip, and lots of names
About the citizens and their doin's.

Ads and subscribers paid the bills.
The little paper grew and grew,
Linotypes, bigger press, more reporters
Covered the county "like the dew."

Change happened over the years,
News now sent through the air,
Blips flashed to electric gadgets
Lured readers away from there.

The paper couldn't keep pace
With computers, blogs, the Internet,
Invisible web turnin' the world
Into a vast buzzin' receivin' set.

Residents of the town now get
News on a glowin', flickerin' screen.
Hometown coverage has been reduced.
Local events and names seldom seen.

The old cattle trail faded away
Into the distant mist of history.
The paper followed a similar path,
And "30" marked end of story.

To Ride
The River With

"He'll do to ride the river with,"
The highest praise to be paid,
A phrase that's part of cowboy myth,
A compliment, the best accolade.

"Where'd that sayin' come from?"
The boy asked old Uncle John,
Who'd been wild and adventuresome
As a cowboy in Texas and Oregon.

"Well, I was there at the time
When that expression was born,
Back when I was in my prime,
When we hired the Waco greenhorn."

The boy was thrilled to hear a tale
About those long-ago years
Workin' cattle on the Chisholm Trail,
Pushin' north those longhorn steers.

Uncle John had been prone
To stretch the truth occasionally,
But he'd also been known
To tell it like it used to be.

"'Twas the CR herd," Uncle John said,
"Rounded up down Goliad way,
Up the trail with two thousand head
One of the first, or so they say.

"Past Fort Worth, we drove 'em hard,
All the way up to Red River Station,
Always alert and ever on guard,
Bein' one man short an irritation.

"That's why the old trail boss
Decided to hire the kid from Waco
To ride drag and help us cross
The river, quicksand and undertow.

"The Red had flooded but was droppin'.
We waited two days, but the boss said go,
So we started yellin' and whoopin',
Crowded the lead steers into the flow.

"We got some to the other side,
Cattle, horses, cowboys in the water;
Waco at the rear, lookin' wild-eyed,
But clingin' on like a real bronc buster.

"Only heads, horns and bulgin' eyes
Showed above the churnin' surface,
When I heard several loud cries.
Don't let 'em stall and stop in place.

"One lead steer started circlin'
In the middle of the rushin' torrent;
The herd followed and was swingin',
A strugglin' mass panicked and violent.

"Cattle crowded, some pushed down
In a confused flounderin' commotion,
Many of the beasts about to drown,
Cowboys, horses caught in the whirlin' motion.

"Suddenly, a cowboy in his underwear
Swam his horse, showin' no fear,
Jumped right onto the cattle swimmin' there,
Walked on their backs to the big lead steer.

"'Twas greenhorn Waco crossin' the pack,
The cowboys all shouted in surprise;
Waco leaped on the big steer's back,
All we could do was watch and agonize.

"Waco pulled on the horns some more,
The big steer thrashed a bit and then
Turned, headin' for the north shore
Followed by the herd, horses and men.

"Cowboys scrambled to hold the herd;
Waco jumped off as cowboys cheered.
That's when that sayin' first was heard;
The trail boss all wet and mud-smeared,

"Rode up and pointin' at Waco,
'He'll do to ride the river with.'"
So that's how the phrase came to show
A real top-hand, part of cowboy myth.

Up The Trail
One More Time

"I want to go up the trail once more,"
The old cowboy said, "And do it all before
They shut 'er down for good.
I want to ride the brush, roundin' up longhorns
Brandin' 'em, gatherin' 'em, chasin' 'em in the thorns,
Workin' at my livelihood.

"Boots, spurs, ropes and wide-brimmed hats,
Fightin' dust, coyotes, snakes and bobcats,
I want to do it all again.
Feel the hot Texas sun hard on my face,
Movin' the herd to the next beddin' place,
No matter hail, rain or wind.

"I'd ride point, swing, flank or even drag,
Pushin' 'em past every turn, twist and snag,
Keepin' 'em pointed north
Through storm, river flood, angry stampede,
Strivin', tryin' our level best to succeed
In always goin' forth

"Up the Chisholm to the Kansas pens,
I yearn to go where the long trail ends.
Once more the wild cowtown,
Saloon, dance hall women and gamblin' den,
Cowboys rip-roarin' with a touch of sin,
Afore my final restin' ground."

Willie Sid
The Fastest Gun

You've heard of Billy the Kid,
Sam Bass, Frank and Jesse James,
But have you heard of Willie Sid,
The fastest gun on the Plains.

Willie Sid was so fast with a gun,
He'd beat himself to the draw
In the mirror just for fun
While onlookers gasped in awe.

Rapid like lightnin' from the sky,
Faster than a cat could wink,
Quicker than an eagle's eye,
Swifter than a rattler's blink.

Willie Sid's gun was fast, you see,
All the cowboys around Pecos said,
So you wonder how it came to be
That Willie Sid ended up dead.

He'd killed nine men, and maybe more.
His fame as the fastest gun around
Was becomin' part of Western lore
When a stranger drifted into town.

The stranger said he'd heard of Willie Sid,
And right away issued a warnin'.
He was a gunslinger, that's what he did,
And Willie Sid better be gone by mornin'.

Willie Sid sneered that he'd add a notch
To his gun afore the day was lost,
But in a deadly game you'd better watch
That i's are dotted and t's are crossed.

All the bystanders readily agree,
Willie Sid was the fastest gun that day,
His draw so fast 'twas hard to see
After he stopped to make his play.

Willie Sid and the stranger strode to meet
Face-to-face under the hot Texas sun;
Willie Sid lay dead in the Pecos street.
He forgot to put bullets in his gun.

Wire

They rolled him out into the sun
By the wall at the nursin' home;
His mind wandered and he babbled
About old days bein' free to roam
Brush and grasslands down south,
O'er rollin' hills and plains
North to the Kansas cowtowns
Through heat, hail and blindin' rains.

The nurses listened to his stories
When he rambled about the longhorn
And the big drives up the Chisholm,
Vanished times to lament and mourn;
He made the long trail for 20 years
Before the towns spread like fire,
Before settlers, plows and farms,
Before the comin' of the wire.

He recalled the big roundups,
From San Angelo to Waco,
Longhorns gathered into a flood
From the Brazos to the Frio;
With memories dim and fadin',
He talked of drivin' 'em north,
Three thousand head, a windin' herd,
On the move past old Fort Worth.

They smiled at his fumbled words
When he told of crossin' rivers, streams,
Open country for a thousand miles —
Was it yesterday or just in his dreams?
From the Rio Grande up to Abilene,
Across the Red to Old Duncan Store,
Stampedes, storms, dust and wind,
Monument Hill and hardships by the score.

He was almost a hundred, they said,
Listenin' to his tales of the Washita,
Dover Station, Rush Creek and Silver City,
Cimarron quicksand and ragin' Arkansas;
But the worst of the problems
That brought an end to the trail by far,
The greatest tragedy, he sadly cried,
Was no doubt the comin' of the wire.

Caldwell, Hays and Dodge City, too,
He tried to make 'em understand
That he'd taken part in a great enterprise,
Important, excitin', majestic and grand;
Millions of cattle pushed up the trail,
Adventure, more than you could desire,
Creatin' legends and myths galore,
Before the comin' of the wire.

PART TWO

Musings, Reflections
And Observations

Anger

Anger came upon me today.
It didn't come on little cat feet;
It burst full-blown, and on its way
Brought heat and a faster heartbeat.

The guy cut me off, the danged cuss,
And zoomed into my parking spot.
He drove a shiny new Lexus,
While my truck was old and shot.

He gave me a scornful look
As he hurried into the store,
And left me danglin' on the hook
As I went drivin' around some more.

Wealth, status and privilege
Always seem to rule the roost.
To think otherwise is sacrilege,
So in this case I deduced

His errand was more important
Than what I planned to do,
His rush was more significant
And there was no need to argue.

They say get even and not mad;
I thought about this Lexus bloke,
And an old bumper sticker that I had
In my truck given me as a joke.

I never put it on my old truck
'Cause some of the boys round here
Might object, and it'd be my luck
To meet one with humor elsewhere.

So I stuck it on his rear bumper.
I figured with his rank and class,
He wouldn't mind its bluster,
"For Sure, I Can Kick Your Ass."

At Wal-Mart

On the bench at Wal-Mart,
Watchin' people come and go,
Pushin' carts packed with stuff
That must really make 'em grow —
'Cause some of 'em, more'n a few,
Grown so much they're big as two.

Black Widow

I bent to turn off my water valve,
Lifting the lid and reaching down,
When I was startled by hangin' there
A black widow spider shiny and round.

Red spots and dark ebony shape
Flashed a warnin' and a quick alarm,
Caused me to jump and swiftly pull
My hand from the spidery harm.

The black widow twitched a little in the web,
But did not flee, made barely a motion
Wonderin', I suppose, what tasty morsel
Disturbed its lair with this commotion.

The eerie creature had a strange beauty,
Legs spread, waitin' for its next prey
To enter the tangled, snarled silken trap
To grab and bind and drain its life away.

The menacingly plump eight-legged female,
Devoted to survival, a marvel of evolution,
With deadly look and huntin' skills,
Filled me with morbid dreadful caution.

She eats flies, mosquitos, bugs and beetles,
Other spiders, her own babies and her lover
In gruesome, gory and horrible manner,
Her reputation grim, cruel and sinister.

I hesitated, but I knew for certain
I had to kill her, but I don't know why
It struck me as peculiar that her existence
Meant many, many victims had to die.

I'm definitely not a member of PETA,
Don't care much about animal rights,
And I assuredly don't have qualms
About spiders or any such critter that bites.

I thought about death and mortality,
The struggles over the eons of mankind,
How maybe we weren't too far apart
This little killer and my own kind.

I smashed her with a pointed stick;
She was blockin' what I had to do.
She was a vicious killer, that is true,
But remember, my race is a killer, too.

Brother David

Brother David was a righteous man
Who preached the gospel to one and all,
With shouts and cries and tearful prayers,
Pleading for sinners to obey the call.

He told of eternal burnin' in hell,
How they had to change their ways,
Give up their evil deeds and prepare
To meet the Lord in the final days.

Stop breakin' commandments, he warned,
Turn away from wickedness and sin,
Start followin' the words of the Good Book,
Now was the time for true faith to begin.

That's why it came as quite a shock
When Brother David one summer day,
Stole the money from the building fund,
And with the church secretary ran away.

Casino

Don't you understand?
I can win it all back
On the very next hand.

    But you've lost the rent,
    And the grocery money, too.
    Your paycheck is spent.

You don't seem to understand.
All that I really need
Is to play another hand.

    No, I will not loan you
    Any more money now,
    No matter what you say or do.

But you don't understand,
I know I can win,
If I play just one more hand.

Change

Bein' old and set in my ways,
There's some things I don't care for —
Cell phones, computers and such
I find mighty easy to ignore.

But I keep bumpin' into Change
All around me night and day;
Tho I say, "Don't bother me,"
Change keeps gettin' in my way.

In many forms and guises,
Roughin' me up in ways most strange,
I find myself unable to escape
The only permanence: Change.

Chewin' and Dippin'

She said, "I've had enough
Your chewin' tobacco
And dippin' snuff.
The spit cans have to go.
Those habits are vile,
I can't stand it anymore.
You've gotta quit, or I'll
Be goin' out the door."

He said, "Okay, but you too
Have to give up somethin'
That's irritatin' in my view —
Like naggin' and gossipin'
And primpin' for too long
When we're goin' somewhere;
It wouldn't be at all wrong
For you to change, fair is fair."

So he's still chewin' and dippin',
And she's still naggin',
Gossipin' and primpin'.
All the neighbors and kin
Say they're gettin' along,
Livin' in blessed harmony;
Live and let live's their song —
And they're singin' it jointly.

Culture

"The only culture here is agriculture,"
the back-East visitor had to say.
"There's no art that's mature,
And certainly no opera or ballet."

We said there's art in the sunset sky,
Opera in the wind through the trees,
Ballet in the dance of the butterfly,
And music in the sound of the honeybees.

Drink

He was drinkin' Lone Star
In a dark Fort Worth bar;
Wasted, he said, I've wasted my life,
Lost my job, family and wife,
Been to rehab and the 12 steps,
Nothin', nothin' ever helps.
Drink used to help me cope,
And once it gave me hope
That I could handle anxiety,
And fears that possessed me.
Drownin' my sorrows, and I quote,
Don't help 'cause sorrows float.
Troubles dim for a little while
Then they're back hauntin' and vile.
I start now early in the day,
Tryin' to drink the agony away.
What I seek, what I crave
Is the silence of the grave.

Dyin' Small Towns

"This is the richest, greatest country
In all the world," we often hear.
Perhaps 'tis true, but in some small towns,
Crumblin', dyin', beginning to disappear,
Another story is bein' told and retold
Of failed hopes and broken dreams,
Paint-peelin' houses, boarded-up stores,
Aftermath of a disaster, or so it seems.

Schools, churches once were thrivin' out here
In the little farm towns on the Plains;
Now fewer farmers, but bigger farms,
People fleein' poverty and misery's pains.
Old cars, pickup trucks parked in yards,
Rusted tractors, plows, obsolete hayrakes;
Some old people keep hangin' on;
Offspring, doctors, grocers pullin' up stakes.

In the little towns not much remains,
Desolate, decayin' from Canada to Texas;
Life up and down the heartland Plains
Drains away like sand through an hourglass.
Businesses closed, ruins all down Main Street,
Boarded up, leanin', wasted, fallin' down,
Windows broken out, no buyers anywhere
For abandoned structures of the rural meltdown.

These little towns were founded originally
By hardy pioneers with strong work ethic;
Country settled by hardworkin' families
Glad to be buildin' a future brick by brick.
Great Depression, World Wars, bigger machines,
Consolidated, improved methods of agriculture,
Fewer and fewer people livin' on the land;
Urban centers pullin' the young with bright allure.

Still open maybe a single grain elevator,
Convenience store/gas station, perhaps a bank,
Post office, a shrinkin' school, antique shops,
Scattered around a tall, tarnished water tank.
Bringin' the end to an American way of life,
The slow death of the small farm town,
Some things lost forever, and all that's left behind
Are despair and the wind's lonely sound.

Empties

The boy sprawled lookin' at the sky,
Big white fluffy clouds rollin' by.
His grandpa said, "Empties goin' to the Gulf,
And when they get moisture enough,
They'll come back this way again.
We'll get another chance for rain then.
What goes around, comes around."
The boy watched the "empties" south bound
With hopeful expectation,
Contemplation and anticipation.

First Day
of School

I passed a slow school bus
As I drove along a country road,
And a little girl waiting by the drive
Slumped like she carried a heavy load.

Tears were shiny on her cheeks,
A pretty dress and bright hairpin.
I smiled because I knew
School's first day, must've been.

Back up the drive beside a bush
A woman with a switch I saw
Stern, grim, determined scowl,
No doubt the poor girl's Ma.

First grade jitters, I suppose
Created this little roadside scene —
The girl facing what to her
Seemed a world scary and mean.

Don't know why this picture
Stands out so sharp for me,
Perhaps it calls back the time
I made a similar journey.

What would it be like,
This dreaded first school day?
Exciting, thrilling, confusing,
Or maybe full of cheery play?

Would I know what to do,
Or how to stand or where to go?
And what if the teacher asked
Something that I didn't know?

These same anxieties I find,
And even more troubling fears,
Have followed like a shadow
As I travel through the years.

Giant Windmills

Standin' along the ridge
White against the sky
Arms outstretched acatchin'
Wind blowin' from on high.

Like wavin' scarecrows
Flailin' through the air
Singin' a noisy song
Sendin' power everywhere.

Sentinels on guard
Lined up in a row,
Signposts to mark
Progress down below.

Gloomy Day

"'Twas a dark and gloomy day,"
'Tis a terrible, terrible cliché,
All the writin' critics say.

But on a day like today,
Pourin' rain and skies are gray,
Can words be used a better way?

Gray Boy

I was seven in the summer of
'43,
War raging with Japan and
Germany;
Me and my little friends were
aware
Of the fierce fighting over
there.

Shockin' news about the
enemy
Was sternly and firmly
relayed to me —
"German POWs from the
Army base
Are choppin' cotton at
Granny's place."

I was warned to stay away
From the cotton field that day,
But from the corner of a big
haystack
Close to the fence by Granny's
shack,

I watched the POWs in the
field,
Makin' sure I was concealed;
There was an Army truck,
driver, guard,
And about ten prisoners
workin' hard.

Each had "PW" stenciled on
his shirt,
A straw hat, a hoe, diggin' in
the dirt
Up and down the cotton row,
'Neath Oklahoma sun,
bendin' low.

Driver and guard stayed in
the shade
While I made sure no prisoner
strayed;
I knew they were probably
spies
Wantin' to escape from under
our eyes.

Now, Granny's dog was big
and gray,
Part German shepherd, I'd
heard them say.
Gray Boy's rules were swift
and strict:
All critters and strangers he'd
evict;

Those he didn't know were
barred
From Granny's little house
and yard,
But I could pull his tail and
ear,
Wrestle him around with no
fear.

A prisoner headed for the
well,
I didn't know if I should run
or yell.
Gray Boy growled and
snarled,
Neck hair bristled, his lips
curled.

The prisoner motioned like he
was drinkin'
From the well, but I was
thinkin',
"Here it is, he's tryin' to flee
And go on some awful evil
spree."

"Goot Hund," it sounded like
he said
To Gray Boy, who slightly
shook his head.
His ears were flat, his teeth
showin'.
The prisoner slowed, but he
kept goin'.

He's speaking German, I
realized,
And I was almost paralyzed —
Gray Boy was German —
German shepherd!!
It was the craziest thing I ever
heard.

Gray Boy might just join their
side,
And then maybe he would
decide
To help them in some terrible
way,
Although how I couldn't
really say.

The prisoner kept on repeatin'
"Goot Hund," like a clever
greetin',
With a strange and foreign
accent
That caused me more torment.

Was it some secret spoken
command
That only Gray Boy would
understand?
But Gray Boy crouched low
and sprang
Growling, snarling with
snapping fang.

I called his name, Gray Boy
stopped.
The German grabbed the hoe
he'd dropped,
And then he quickly wisely
chose
To scurry back to the cotton
rows.

Granny told me later like a
sermon,
"Gray Boy don't speak any
German,
He speaks Okie, and
remember he is true
To the old Red, White and
Blue."

Great Plains

The great sweep
Of the Great Plains,
The great heart
Of the Heartland,
From the tree line
Up in Canada
To the mountains
Down in Mexico.
The strong center
Of the country,
Harsh winds,
Blistering heat,
Flood, drought,
Insects, wildfires,
The Bread Basket
Of the world,
Sea of grass,
Waves of wheat,
Grain elevators,
Cattle herds
On the prairie,
Fences, windmills,
Bustin' the sod,
Years of struggle,
Hard to tame,
Bountiful now
The "fruited plain."
May it always be.

Homesick
For West Texas

He'd spent years up north,
And said he was homesick for:
Sand dunes and lizards,
Gila monsters and rattlesnakes,
Tumbleweeds and wind,
Mesquites and shimmerin' heat,
Blowin' dust and prickly pear
And cholla cactus.

And even for:
Drillin' rigs and pumpjacks,
Derricks and drill bits,
Sucker rods and hoists,
Cables and drillin' mud,
Pipeyards and storage tanks
And well casings.

Ice and Sleet and Snow

Ice and sleet and snow
Fell durin' the night,
A glistenin' shinin' world
Reflected in frosty sunlight.

Tree limbs creaked and moaned
Under their coat of ice,
Icicles dripped off the roof,
Gripped in a wintry vise.

Water heated to thaw the pump,
Poppin' open the cellar lock,
Chickens fed with scattered grain,
Hay tossed for hungry livestock.

Wind softly driftin' past
The fields, woods and hills,
Gloves, boots and heavy coats
Donned to block icy chills.

The dog huddles under the porch,
Smoke curls above the trees
From a neighbor's chimney stack,
Fightin' off the winter freeze.

Breakin' ice on the pond
So thirsty cattle can get a drink,
Turnin' up the propane heat,
Lots of time to sit and think.

Frozen silence o'er the land,
Glitterin' sparklin' diamond scenes
Flashin' through the shortened hours
That the sun sharply gleans.

The cold and white reveal
That Autumn has gone away,
And Spring is yet to come
To break Winter's dreary sway.

We think of those asleep
In the cemetery down the way,
Tombstones topped in ivory white,
Leanin' into the blustery day.

A shroud has fallen down,
A blanket on the countryside,
Another stage, another phase
Of earth's — and man's — timeless tide.

Love Is Blind

Love is blind
And cannot see
Usually.

Lust is blind
And cannot see
Temporarily.

Melancholy

When the melancholy blues
At times descend upon me,
And the dreary moods refuse
To depart and set me free,

When for no reason I can tell,
I feel empty and sorrow-worn,
In order to break the doleful spell
And pierce the gloom forlorn,

I ride out along the ridge
Where the oaks and cedars grow
Forming a green and leafy bridge
Leading away from torment and woe.

I don't know what it is
About this little jaunt of mine,
But nature speaks to me and says,
"You don't need pills, beer or wine

"To get rid of your somberness,
You only need to feast your eye
On the scenery's quiet loveliness
And tell the sadness good-bye."

Our modern lives entrap us,
Put up a strong and sturdy wall
That blocks any natural stimulus
To help us hear serenity's call.

We need to take the time
To connect with earthly things,
To feel and hear the song and rhyme
That Mother Nature sings.

Mockingbird

Mockingbird, oh mockingbird,
Outside my windowsill
Running through your song list
With twitter, chatter and trill.

Cheery call of the robin,
Cawing of the crow,
Cooing of the dove,
Chirp of the sparrow,

Stolen songs singing all alone
Do you have a song
That's your very own?

Morality

Morality,
Hypocrisy —
Close as they can be.
Whose morality?
Whose hypocrisy?
"Who" is the key frequently.

Move On

Do what you have to do,
And move on!
No matter what misfortunes befall you,
See what needs to be done,
Don't wallow in things that are gone.
Do what you have to do
And move on!

Rocky may be the road ahead,
Bleak and grim could be the view,
Shrug off gloom, despair and dread,
Do what you have to do
And move on!

Your ponds may go dry,
Dig a well — you've got to try —
When cattle prices drop,
Keep on hangin' on — don't stop.
Your garden won't grow.
But troubles do, row on row,
Do what you have to do
And move on!

My Cat

My cat naps on the porch,
Doesn't need sleepin' pills,
Not worried about ambition,
Failure, goals or utility bills.

Nine lives, some people say,
The Turks say six, Spanish seven,
Sacred worship in old Egypt
Must have been feline heaven.

No wonder he's aloof and regal;
All those lives and hero worship,
A past steeped in myth and legend,
Boosts his ego better'n catnip.

Old Ben

If Ben Franklin returned today,
He'd be amazed at the way
Technology has changed the world
And all manner of advances unfurled.

Old Ben's favorite business
That brought him fame and happiness,
Publishing has seen dazzlin' change
And he would surely find it strange —

No lead type or presses run by hand;
He'd find it hard to understand
Super-fast printing, computerized type
And transformation of every stripe.

But he'd probably wonder why
As innovative marvels multiply,
Humans in brainpower, wisdom and wit
Have not increased even a little bit.

On Death

Death rides a pale horse,
Carries a scythe sharp and long,
Sometimes a blessing,
Sometimes a sad, mournful song.

Perhaps in swift dramatic strife
Or like sand slowly falling
Quietly through an hourglass,
The Grim Reaper comes calling.

He comes once for all of us,
His visit may be gentle or rough;
One time with this visitor
Is more than enough.

Out Between
The Beaver Creeks

I took a drive out through
The country where I was raised,
Past the old home place all covered
Now in brush, shrub and trees,
Familiar places overgrown and obscured.

Out between the Beaver Creeks,
Past what used to be my Grandpa's farm,
Empty after all these many years,
Down the rutted red-dirt road
Where my uncles, aunts, cousins once lived,
Through the thickly wooded bottomland
Where my Granny's two-room shack stood.

Cotton, corn, wheat and gardens once grew,
Along with cows, pigs, chickens and turkeys, too.
Sharecroppers, dirt poor, hardscrabble and hard up.
Too down-and-out to pull up stakes,
Quit the Dust Bowl and go California way.

Stayed behind when all the rest headed west
In old jalopies loaded with kids, wash tubs,
Mattresses, worn-out debris left from years
Of tryin' to scratch out a livin'
From the Oklahoma dirt.

I drove the narrow roads,
Red sticky mud when it rained,
Blowin' dust and rough most of the time,
Between weed-choked ditches
Filled with sunflowers, Johnson grass.

Two miles to the little school,
Where I trudged to and fro each day,
Nothin' left but a concrete cellar full of water.
No electricity, no indoor plumbing,
Heat from coal and wood-burnin' stoves,
Water from a pump and cistern;

Two outhouses — one for boys and one for girls.
Scraggly swings, seesaws and basketball goal
On a dirt-packed bare playground.
One teacher for eight grades,
Only 15 students when it closed.

Lookin' back, it seemed at the time
Like a permanent world — family all around,
But change was workin' hard —
Depression, Dust Bowl, World War Two,
And a great migration of people out;
My kinfolks all died or moved away.

I, too, left years and years ago
For the cities and the towns,
Tryin' to leave the country ways behind,
Traveled far and wide around the world;
Time tumblin', fleetin', speedin' away,
Bringin' change, with its toll,
The clock turnin' and turnin'.

One thing that leaps out at me,
One thing that I discovered
On this trip into the past:
No matter how long the years,
Or how far away I go,
I will forever be
Down the dusty lane at twilight
That barefoot boy hurrying home.

Rain

Where've you been?
You ain't been here
Since I don't know when —
Pastures all sere,
Creeks all dry;
Don't stay away,
And come back by
Most any day.

Section 23

The pioneer received the land
In the lottery of August 1901,
Brought his young wife down
In a wagon under the summer sun.

Fenced and plowed up the sod,
Built a house, barn and wearily
Fought the bugs, drought and heat
Barely made a livin' on Section 23.

Raised crops and lots of kids,
Backbreaking work filled the day;
Cows, pigs and chickens, too,
Tryin' anything that might pay.

Life was tough and hard-scrabble;
The same was true or even more
Across the rutted dusty road
For the neighbors in Section 24.

But in 24 one fine day, a drillin' rig,
Derrick, machines, cables and crew
Began to bore into the earth
Diggin' down like a giant corkscrew.

The pioneer was younger then,
Rode his horse over to see
What progress was bein' made,
Hopin' maybe they'd drill in 23.

Maybe you can guess the rest;
They hit flowin', roarin' gushers
In several different places;
Pumpjacks now group in clusters.

The dirt-poor settlers of 24
Moved to town, bought a mansion,
Offspring became bank directors,
Partners in wealth expansion.

Trust funds and Cadillacs,
First-class travel and hotel,
Rubbin' elbows with the rich,
Livin' large and livin' well.

While across the way in 23
Efforts made in '31, '35, '42
Turned out to be dry holes;
Nothin' when they were through.

Call it fate, luck or whatever,
Black gold flowed in one spot,
While nearby across the road
Workin' hard was what they got.

The children from that farm
Grew up, prospered to a degree,
But I think the story's a sad one —
My Grandpa owned Section 23.

Sunrise

Sunrise comes on,
No matter our worries;
Every day a new dawn,
And bright hope carries
Troubles away for an instant;
We feel the world reborn,
Fire and gold predominant,
Heralding the coming morn.
Resurrection creating again
Making over once more
A new path to begin
Through the day's door.

Superhero

With a towel my mother gave me
Tied around my neck,
I was a superhero running free
Out where the chickens peck.

I was Batman and Superman
And Captain Marvel, too,
From where the creek ran
To the cottonwood slough.

I captured bad guys left and right
All around the farm,
Fightin' crime day and night
Keepin' the world from harm.

What a simple world I lived in,
In those days long ago.
I caught bad guys back then,
When I was a superhero.

"Take Bob"

They buried my brother today
In the cold Georgia clay.
Thoughts crowded my mind,
Reflections all intertwined.

But I don't know why
One image in my mind's eye
Stands out strong and clear
From all those of yesteryear.

Recollections from back then
Of those olden times when
Sometimes I wanted to go
To the park or the movie show.

"Take Bob," Mom would say,
And I'd whine my dismay,
"Aw, do I have to?"
I had other things to do

That seemed to be better
Than acting as a baby-sitter.
"He just gets in the way,"
My annoyance I'd convey.

I'd pedal our old bike,
Bob would cling glue-like
Holdin' to the handlebars
As we passed potholes, cars.

"Watch out for your brother,"
Admonition from my mother.
Bob was a little shaver,
And I was six years older.

Now as I stand by his grave
Feelings like a tidal wave
Come flooding over me.
If only I had the ability

To hear just once more
Mom say, "And furthermore,
Take Bob with you."
And that's what I'd do.

I'd take him on a ride
To places far and wide,
I would never complain
If I could do it all again.

That's Entertainment

When did Entertainment
Become a big part of everything?
It's always been around,
But today it's overwhelming.
Was it when radio emerged
With sounds filling the air?
"Jack Armstrong" and "Fibber McGee"
And songs and jokes everywhere?

Or movies, silent and then talkies,
Flickering black and white,
Escapism, diversion and titillation
Fed the growing appetite.
Show Biz and Hollywood,
Headlines filled by celebrity;
Television burst upon the scene,
"I Love Lucy" and "Howdy Doody."

Now blogs and Twitter and Internet
And all sorts of amusement
Floating around to be picked
By some gadget from the firmament
Like ripe berries from the vine;
Politicians have to "entertain,"
So do teachers and preachers—
Laughs and good times reign.

"Boring, boring" becomes the kiss
Of death for any and all.
Kids want to be "entertained"
And adults, too, heed the call.
Seriousness gets pushed aside,
Depth and detail lost in the fun,
Information must be sugar-coated,
Or it fades into oblivion.

Thought, meditation, reflection
Reduced in the rush for recreation.
So what's the cure for the problem?
Some say it has to be education —
But the Entertainment snowball
Keeps rolling faster and faster —
Are we going to win the race
Between education and disaster?

The Plumber
Came Today

The plumber came today,
Repaired the clogged-up line,
Didn't charge too awful much
If you own a big gold mine.

The old outhouse on the farm,
Lackin' any allure or charm,
Was rustic, primitive and crude;
Fixin' didn't cost a leg and arm.

The Storm

Clouds dark and swirlin'
Came across the prairie sky
Ominous, threatenin' and roilin',
Puttin' anxiety levels on high.
Rumblin' down tornado alley
Where twisters often roam,
And storms not taken lightly
By those who call it home.
Lightnin' crashed, thunder rolled,
Rain came down in a flood,
Nature's fury to behold,
Turnin' country roads to mud.
Fear sent people hurryin'
To safety, shelters, cellars,
Nervous, tense and worryin'
About kids, houses, cars.
Then sunshine breakin' through,
Storms clouds goin' away,
Calm returns as they knew
Sweet relief for another day.

The Universe

This old cowboy finds it hard
To grasp what scientists now say
Are the latest amazin' avant-garde
Findings about the universe today.

Once we thought the earth
Was the center of everything,
Then the solar system held forth,
Then our Milky Way galaxy was king.

Then discoveries upon discoveries,
And stunnin' revelations made it clear
Billions and billions of galaxies
Filled our universe far and near.

And now wonder upon wonder,
They say our gigantic universe,
And this really makes me ponder,
May be just part of a multiverse —

Billions, billions and billions more
Of universes like our very own,
Where our earth barely accounts for
A small dot in an unremarkable zone.

Our importance and significance
Shrink away to almost nothin'
With every fact and circumstance
Astronomers keep on unravelin'.

I can't help but be in awe
As I stare up at the starry sky,
And ask if it could be a basic law
That other earths might occupy

Those worlds and like this one
There might be hard-ridin' cowhands
Toilin' under a boilin' sun
Pushin' a herd through alien lands.

We might think that mighty odd,
But things get bizarre and strange,
Some might even say whopper-jawed,
Way out on that celestial range.

The Wichitas

The ancient Wichitas,
500 million years old,
Worn by eternal laws
Volcano-hot, ice-age cold.

The oldest mountains
In all the world,
The granite rock sustains
Pink cliffs all unfurled.

The once towering peaks,
Whittled by nature's fury,
Call to one who seeks
A place of continuity

Amid the ebb and flow,
Frantic hurried changes
Of a world on the go
That rushin' time arranges.

Indians called it home
Long before white traders
And settlers began to roam
Around its stony borders.

Thrustin' toward the sky
From gentle rollin' plains,
The beauty warms the eye
Through sun, wind and rains.

Red granite cobblestones,
Rounded boulders everywhere,
Flowers of various tones,
Goldenrod and prickly pear,

Cedars, blackjack oak,
Willows and cottonwood,
Mist like driftin' smoke
Engulf the quiet solitude.

Legends and stories abound
About the rugged ravines
Of gold buried in the ground
By Kiowas and Comanches.

Other Indian raiders, too,
Along the Chisholm and Santa Fe
Could hide out and renew
To ride again another day.

Frank and Jesse James,
Or so the stories say
And the legacy proclaims,
Left loot unfound to this day.

The Wichitas' dramatic lore
Continues over the years,
Minin' precious ore
Booms, then disappears.

Quanah and Geronimo
Spent their final days
In the mountains' shadow,
Closin' out the old ways.

Now the abidin' summits
Are part of a preserve
That guards and permits
Creatures a safe reserve.

Buffalo and longhorn,
Both close to extinction,
Herds have been reborn
Rescued from oblivion.

Elk and white-tailed deer,
And other wildlife, too,
Flourish and widely appear
Allowed to begin life anew

In the vast refuge haven
Created as a protected shelter
Set aside and then given
To the nation to last forever.

And the perpetual crests'
Stunnin' scenery graces
One of the Southwest's
Most endurin' places.

The Wind

The Oklahoma wind is always there;
We're raised from babies quite aware
Of whisperin' when it kissed a tree,
Or screamin' as it swept the prairie.
Hotter than a furnace's blast,
Or icy when skies are overcast;
Blowin' at your back or in your face,
Movin' with you from place to place;
Nature's reminder, I dare say,
That things don't always go your way.

Time

I met Time on the highway,
"You're goin' faster and faster
The older I get," I say.
"What can I do to make
Time slow down or stay?"
Time stared blankly at me,
And then hurried on his way.

Tornado

Way out here on the plains
When you think you're significant,
That you're a big shot of great import,
That your status is predominant—

You're the top dog of your pack,
Your bank account is big and fat,
And you're healthy, wealthy and wise—
You strut your stuff and all that,

Nature can whittle you down to size,
And can quickly and firmly show
That you're not so awful much
Wrapped in the arms of a tornado.

True Love

Love, the kind that lasts and abides,
The kind that is deep and true,
Certain, faithful, patient, strong,
That's the kind I have for you.

Love that endures and remains,
The kind that turmoil won't undo
Despite the storms that life brings,
That's the kind I have for you.

Love that grows over the years,
The kind that blooms and flowers anew
With ups and downs, twists and turns,
That's the kind I have for you.

Veterans

At a theater up in Branson
During a break in song and fun,

Those who served the nation
In peacetime or at a battle station

Were asked to stand to be recognized
For keeping the country free and civilized.

Wouldn't it make far more sense
For veterans of sea, land and air defense

To keep their seats in restful attitude
While others stood to show their gratitude?

"We Will Endure"

The twister hit the trailer park,
Wreckage and debris everywhere,
Houses blown apart, three killed,
Devastation, tragedy hung in the air.

A woman sobbed amid the ruin,
Holding a torn, muddy photo
Pulled from out the rubble,
"We will endure, this we know."

CPSIA information can be obtained at www.ICGtesting.com
Printed in the USA
LVOW102252080712

289227LV00001B/2/P